ELT Development Series

SERIES EDITOR Thomas S. C. Farrell

Teaching English for Specific Purposes

Vander Viana, Ana Bocorny, and Simone Sarmento

www.tesol.org/bookstore

TESOL International Association
1925 Ballenger Avenue
Alexandria, Virginia, 22314 USA
www.tesol.org

Director of Publishing and Product Development: Myrna Jacobs
Copy Editor: Sarah J. Duffy
Cover: Citrine Sky Design
Interior Design & Layout: Capitol Communications, LLC
Printing: Gasch Printing, LLC

Every effort has been made to contact copyright holders for permission to
reprint borrowed material. We are grateful to thyssenkrupp Elevator for
allowing us to reproduce a page from one of its elevator manuals in Chapter
4. We regret any oversights that may have occurred and will rectify them in
future printings of this work.

ISBN 978-1-942799-91-7
Library of Congress Control No. 2018952188

Table of Contents

Series Editor's Preface

The English Language Teacher Development (ELTD) series consists of
a set of short resource books for ESL/EFL teachers that are written in a
jargon-free and accessible manner for all types of teachers of English (native,
nonnative, experienced, and novice teachers). The ELTD series is designed
to offer teachers a theory-to-practice approach to second language teaching,
and each book offers a wide range of practical teaching approaches and
methods of the topic at hand. Each book also offers time for reflections for
each teacher to interact with the materials presented in the book. The books
can be used in preservice settings or in-service courses and can also be used
by individuals looking for ways to refresh their practice.

Teaching English for Specific Purposes, by Vander Viana, Ana Bocorny,
and Simone Sarmento, explores various aspects of teaching English for
specific purposes (ESP) and how such an approach can inform language
teaching. Viana, Bocorny, and Sarmento outline why ESP is important, what
ESP is, the different types of ESP, and various materials that can be incor-
porated into an ESP course. The authors also outline such key features of
ESP as needs analysis, genre, specialized vocabulary, and corpus linguistics.
Teaching English for Specific Purposes is another valuable addition to the
literature in our profession and to the ELTD series.

I am very grateful to the authors who contributed to the ELTD series for sharing their knowledge and expertise with other TESOL professionals. It was truly an honor for me to work with each of these authors as they selflessly gave up their valuable time for the advancement of TESOL.

Thomas S. C. Farrell

CHAPTER 1

Introduction

This book focuses on the teaching of English for specific purposes (ESP), which may be a new area within English language teaching (ELT) for you. In order to contextualize our discussion of ESP, the book starts by highlighting the key features of English for general purposes (EGP) and by indicating how ESP differs from it.

English for General Purposes (EGP)

As its name indicates, EGP relates to the mastery of English without any specific use being prioritized. The target to be reached in EGP is students' proficiency, and the focus lies on the development of their general communicative ability.

Several decisions are taken before EGP students enter the classroom. These can be made by governments (e.g., curricular guidelines), language institutes (e.g., identification of the content to be assessed), textbooks (e.g., their language foci), teachers (e.g., their decision of what to teach), and other stakeholders. However, students are not usually consulted; that is, they are not asked why they are learning English and what exactly they want to study, for instance. In some contexts, that is understandable: Asking 5-year-old children how they plan to use English in their lives might be beyond their understanding. The same might not hold true in relation to adults, for example.

EGP curricula are frequently determined a priority—even before students enroll for these courses. Because of their emphasis on general language, EGP courses prioritize interactional and social texts (e.g., face-to-face conversations between two friends, phone exchanges to book a hotel), and they generally focus on the skills of speaking and listening (Hamp-Lyons, 2001).

English for Specific Purposes (ESP)

REFLECTIVE QUESTIONS

- What do you know about ESP?

- How does it differ from other English lessons?

ESP does not aim at improving students' English proficiency indiscriminately. Instead, students are acknowledged as important stakeholders who have decided to study this language for particular reasons. After these reasons are mapped, we, as teachers, can help them reach their goals.

The gold standard in ESP is to allow students to use English to fulfill their needs (e.g., read a manual, write a dissertation, listen to a lecture, present a sales pitch). For example, there is little point in teaching writing to bus drivers in an ESP course. For these professionals, the skills of listening and speaking are probably the most important ones since they will have to interact with passengers (e.g., charge the fare), colleagues (e.g., negotiate their schedule), and police officers (e.g., ask for directions if they come across road diversions).

ESP curricula cannot be predetermined in a social/educational vacuum; they need to be prepared in response to specific contextual factors. The texts to be used in ESP courses are likely to differ widely even when the development of the same skill is being targeted. For instance, ESP writing courses vary depending on the target students: Accountants might need to study financial reports, journalists will need to learn about news stories, and lexicographers should specialize in the writing of dictionary entries. In sum, the texts to be used in ESP should relate to the tasks that the students have to undertake in their daily routines.

Types of ESP

The specific purposes in ESP are generally related to either one's profession or one's academic studies (Dudley-Evans, 2001; Spiro, 2013). The former is referred to as English for occupational purposes (EOP; e.g., English for call center operators, English for bank tellers, English for servers), and the latter is termed English for academic purposes (EAP; e.g., pre- and in-sessional English language support offered at universities where English is the language of instruction).

In this book, we equate ESP with EOP; our discussion centers on the English to be taught so that our students can perform their jobs. There are two reasons for this. First, although EAP is a type of ESP (i.e., the academic purposes being one of the possible special purposes), it has developed as a field of its own. Second, there already is a volume on EAP in this book series (see Kostka & Olmstead-Wang, 2015), which is relevant to those working with university-level students or with students who are planning to join/return to university.

Even if an occupation is specified, there will never be a single ESP course suitable to all professionals in that area. Figure 1 illustrates this in relation to ESP courses in legal English. All of the courses presented in Figure 1 relate to one another, but they differ in their degree of specificity. For example, an ESP course on legal English would not only focus on the needs of solicitors but also have to cater for judges, barristers, attorneys general, directors of public prosecutions, and so on. An ESP course for novice solicitors (i.e., those entering the profession) would differ from one

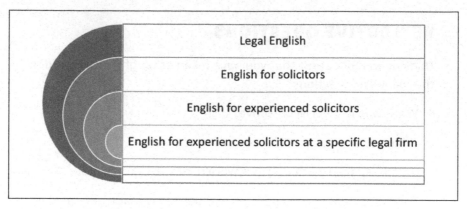

Figure 1: From General to Specific ESP Courses

for students who already have considerable professional experience. In short, ESP courses can vary in their degree of specialism.

Teachers' and Students' Roles in ESP

While ESP teachers may have some understanding of the fields in which their students work, these teachers do not have to be knowledgeable in all of these fields. A degree in law or medicine is not required of teachers in ESP courses for lawyers or doctors.

In ESP, teachers' and students' roles are different but complementary. Teachers are the language education specialists; they know (about) English in addition to having pedagogical skills. Students, on the other hand, have some knowledge of their professional field (generally in their first language) and usually have a real motivation to learn the language (e.g., communicate with clients, read a manual, be promoted). It is not possible to generalize, however, whether they know English. Liu and Berger (2015) state that ESP students typically have an intermediate or advanced knowledge of English, but this is not always the case. We have been involved in the development of ESP courses where the target students—airline mechanics and bus drivers—had very basic knowledge of English (if any).

Given these profiles, a truly symbiotic relationship can be established in ESP courses. Teachers can learn with their students more about the latter's professional practices, while students can learn how to use English successfully at their workplaces. ESP can therefore be seen as a collaborative partnership where there is a real information gap and a communication need between teachers and students.

Materials in EGP and ESP Courses

One key difference between published EGP and ESP materials is that the former would generally be part of a textbook series while the latter would commonly be gathered in a single textbook. This relates to typical course length: EGP courses last longer than ESP courses. The brief duration of the latter relates to the pressures from the field where the students work—for example, they might need to learn English as soon as possible to be able to get their jobs done, and/or the course might be funded by the employer, who does not want to spend too much money on it.

REFLECTIVE QUESTIONS

Table 1 indicates the contents from the first two units of two textbooks. Study the table carefully and try to answer the following questions.

- Can you identify the EGP and the ESP book?

- Given our discussion so far, how do you justify your answers?

Table 1. Contents From Two Textbooks

Book		A		B	
Reference		Gomm & Hird (2001, p. 7)		MacKenzie (2008, p. 4)	
Unit		1	2	1	2
Topic		"Identity"	"Taste"	"The organization of the financial industry"	"Telephoning"
Skills	Speaking	• "Recognising famous people" • "Discussing what gives you your identity" • "Discussing an ambiguous situation & photographs" • "A telephone conversation" • "Anecdote: talking about your job, home town or family"	• "If you were a food . . ." • "Talking about food associations" • "Discussing good taste" • "Game: expanding sentences" • "Anecdote: describing your favourite restaurant"	• "Role play: Bank account terms and conditions"	• "Role plays: Arranging meetings, Asking for information"

continued on next page

Table 1. *(continued)*

Book		A		B	
Skills *(continued)*	Listening	• "People describing what gives them their identity" • "Song: *My Girl* by Madness" • "Boyfriend & girlfriend arguing on the telephone"	• "People talking about the food they associate with certain situations" • "People describing food experiences abroad" • "Friends discussing good taste"	• "The development of the financial industry; Going international"	• "Arranging meetings; Handling information"
	Reading	• "Extracts from *Men Are From Mars, Women Are From Venus* by John Gray" • "A case of mistaken identity"	• "Article: a restaurant review"	• "Regulation and deregulation"	
	Writing	• "Writing about another student in the class"	• "Writing a restaurant review"		
Systems	Vocabulary	• "Vocabulary of personal values" • "Word building"	• "Taste & its collocations"	• "Key vocabulary of banking products and services"	
	Grammar	• "Adverbials: types and position" • "Phrasal verbs with objects"	• "Describing nouns" • "Order of adjectives" • "Test yourself: past tenses" • "Fronting"	• "Permission, necessity and prohibition"	
	Pronunciation	• "Getting angry"	• "Expressing enthusiasm & reservations" • "Expressions for agreeing & disagreeing"		• "Pronouncing the alphabet and saying telephone numbers"

Even without knowing the book titles (and we hope you did not cheat by looking up the references!), you probably realized that Book A is an EGP textbook—in this case, *Inside Out* (Gomm & Hird, 2001)—while Book B is an ESP textbook—namely, *English for the Financial Sector* (MacKenzie, 2008). Several features support our reasoning, some of which are summarized in Table 1.

Table 2 presents just one example of an ESP book. There is no recipe for what ESP materials should contain and how they should be organized. Their contents and structure are informed by the results of needs analysis, an important step in ESP design that is discussed in Chapter 2.

Table 2. Summary of Differences Between an EGP Textbook and an ESP Textbook

	EGP	ESP
Topics	General life (e.g., identity)	Specific to the occupation (e.g., financial industry)
Skills	Focus on all four skills	Selective emphasis (e.g., writing is not dealt with in the first two units)
Texts	Interactive, social, and informal (e.g., discussions, telephone conversations, introductions, arguments)	Informative (e.g., financial industry development), transactional (e.g., arrangements), and formal (e.g., professional and customer)
Language content	General knowledge of English (e.g., adverbials, order of adjectives)	Key aspects needed for the target professionals (e.g., words related to banking products/services)
Activities	Games, anecdotes, songs	Role-plays

Next Chapters

This introduction focused on the differences between ESP and EGP to help you more fully understand the former. The following five chapters focus solely on ESP. Chapter 2 introduces you to needs analysis, the first step in the development of any ESP course. It details what information you should gather and how you can do so. Chapter 3 explains the concept of genre and illustrates how you can engage in genre-based teaching. Consideration is then given to specialized vocabulary in Chapter 4, which discusses pedagogical matters such as what words/expressions need to be learned, how these can be taught, and how students can develop their lexical knowledge independently. Chapter 5 deals with corpus linguistics, an area that has been the center of attention in ESP (cf. A. M. Johns, 2012). Based on real-life language use, corpus investigations provide ESP teachers with useful patterns to teach in their classes. The sixth and final chapter briefly summarizes the main topics discussed in this book and indicates how you may develop your ESP learning in pedagogical and research terms.

REFLECTIVE QUESTIONS

As you explore the following chapters, keep asking yourself whether/how the suggestions presented in the book

- relate to your experience as an English language teacher, and

- can be implemented in your own teaching context.

CHAPTER 2

Needs Analysis

This chapter explains the importance of needs analysis to the development of ESP courses, illustrates how it relates to language skills, presents some of the sources and methods that can be used to collect data, and suggests how the information collected through needs analysis can be usefully organized.

REFLECTION QUESTIONS

- What is the first thing you do when you are asked to teach a new course?

- To what extent do you consider different stakeholders' views other than yours (e.g., students', parents', employers') when designing your courses?

- What do you know about needs analysis?

Relevance of Needs Analysis

The term *needs analysis*—also referred to as *needs assessment* by Brown (2016)—is used in many different areas (e.g., marketing, business, engineering). In ESP, needs analysis is the first stage in course development

(Flowerdew, 2013). The data collected through needs analysis (e.g., what students need to do with English, what skills and genres need to be mastered) should inform syllabus design and materials development (Hyland, 2006) so that these are aligned with students' needs and profiles as well as with the needs, perceptions, and interests of other stakeholders (e.g., employers, governments, funding bodies).

REFLECTION QUESTIONS

- Have you ever conducted needs analysis?
  - If so, whose perspectives did you take into account? What methods did you use to gather their views? How did you use the data to inform course development?
  - If not, think of a course you are going to teach in the near future and consider (a) whose views you will gather, (b) how you will collect relevant data, and (c) how you will use the data to inform the proposed syllabus.

Needs Analysis and Language Skills

In this section, we consider the example of an ESP course designed for commercial pilots, one of the projects that we have been involved in.

REFLECTION QUESTION

- Which skills (i.e., reading, writing, listening, speaking) would you prioritize in an ESP course for commercial pilots?

You probably thought of speaking as one of the key skills in this ESP course since commercial pilots need to communicate with air traffic controllers (ATCs), for instance. As a matter of fact, per the guidelines defined by the International Civil Aviation Organization (2004), oral proficiency is the main focus of the mandatory proficiency test for these professionals.

While speaking is clearly important for commercial pilots, they do not use English only to communicate with ATCs. They also need to (a) read operations manuals, (b) write discrepancy reports (i.e., reports written by pilots when they note a problem in the aircraft), and (c) listen to automatic terminal information service recordings, that is, "a continuous recorded radio transmission of meteorological conditions at an airport" (Neville, 2004, p. 6).

Sources and Methods in Needs Analysis

REFLECTION QUESTIONS

- What sources do you consult when you have to design a new course from scratch?

- Who do you ask for guidance in the development of a new course?

- Who are the relevant stakeholders in the ESP course that you are planning to design?

- What questions would you ask these stakeholders?

- Which method(s) would you use to collect their views?

Perhaps most of us resort to our own beliefs and intuitions as starting points in ESP course development. Other teachers who have taught similar ESP courses might also come in handy for sharing materials and perceptions.

Given the occupational nature of ESP, experienced professionals could also be consulted to provide a detailed description of the tasks that they perform in English and of the language that they are likely to use. Because ESP students are (future) professionals in the field, they can be resourceful when it comes to providing insider information about their fields of specialization.

Knowing about students' reasons for learning the language is also important. This information can be gathered easily in a get-to-know-you activity at the beginning of the course. Asking ESP students to write a short paragraph about their educational and professional background in English is an informal way of assessing their language proficiency level.

In some cases, what students have to learn might be established by the government or by a funding body. It is therefore important to read documents that describe what is expected of them (see, e.g., International Civil Aviation Organization, 2004, for ESP courses for commercial pilots).

Existing ESP course books can be a source of valuable information. Naturally, with ESP students' potential range of specialisms, what is available on the market will not always match students' needs. In this situation, we can rely on some other useful sources: (a) academic publications (e.g., books, journal articles, PhD theses) on the topic of the course and (b) texts that are produced and/or consumed by professionals in students' field(s) of specialization (see Chapter 5 for more information).

One last source of information can be our own observation of the target situation. Neville (2004), for instance, observed and described the communication between captains and copilots during flights.

Table 3 summarizes the types of information that can be gathered in needs analysis, the likely sources to be examined, the methods that can be employed, and the potential foci of the analyses.

Table 3. Sources, Methods and Foci in Needs Analysis

Information	Sources	Data collection methods	Foci
Domain	Professional contexts (e.g., cockpit of an airplane, car factory, hospital)	● Observations of professional practice	● What tasks are performed in English? ● What skills (i.e., reading, listening, speaking, writing) are required for each task? ● What lexical/grammatical items are used when performing the tasks?
Stakeholders	Students	● Class activities (e.g., get-to-know-you activity) ● Informal conversations ● Questionnaires ● Proficiency test results (e.g., TOEFL, IELTS, more informal ways of assessing students' proficiency) ● Interviews	● What are students' profiles and backgrounds? (e.g., age, nationality, gender, educational background, professional experience, English proficiency level, knowledge of specialized English) ● How have they learned English? ● How do they like to learn English? ● What professional knowledge do they already have? ● What are their perceived job-related learning needs?

continued on next page

Teaching English for Specific Purposes

Table 3. *(continued)*

Information	Sources	Data collection methods	Foci
Stakeholders *(continued)*	Teachers and applied linguists	• Informal conversations with more experienced teachers who have already taught similar courses • Observations of ESP classes • Interviews with more experienced teachers and applied linguists • Questionnaires • Participation in discussion groups or associations like TESOL's English for Specific Purposes Interest Section	• According to teachers and/or applied linguists, what problems do students face when producing/consuming relevant specialized genres? • Which approaches seem to be the most effective in the observed ESP classes or as reported by more experienced teachers/applied linguists?
	Institutions (e.g., employers, governments, regulatory agencies, funding bodies)	• Interviews • Analysis of documents that describe what is expected from a certain group of professionals in terms of language proficiency • Questionnaires	• What genres are perceived as most relevant for professionals? • What skills are valued? • What knowledge is regarded as key by selection and/or promotion panels?
	Professionals	• Informal conversations • Observations of professional practice • Interviews • Questionnaires	• What genres do professionals produce/consume the most? • What skills are needed to perform the job successfully? • What language (e.g., vocabulary, grammar) do professionals need to fulfill their tasks in English?
Available literature	Existing ESP pedagogical materials and academic publications	• Analysis of ESP pedagogical materials • Reading of previous research on relevant professional practices	• What content can be found in relevant ESP materials? • What language/genre features are deemed to be most relevant in specialized communicative target situations?
Target language	Examples of (spoken and/or written) texts to be used by the students in their (current/future) occupations	• Identification and analysis of textual sources that are relevant to students' specialism • Collection of relevant texts—with due ethical permission—during on-site ethnographic work • Compilation and analysis of a small specialized corpus (see Chapter 5)	• What genres do professionals in the field need to produce and/or understand? • What rhetorical moves are typical of these genres? • What (sequences of) language items are most commonly found (in the genres and in the moves)? • How are sentences structured and combined?

Organization of Needs Analysis Data

Although the process of data collection for needs analysis can be both tiring and time-consuming, it is essential to organize the information gathered. Doing so will make it easier to use the data to design appropriate course syllabi and materials.

Imagine that you have been invited to teach a preservice ESP course on writing discrepancy reports and your students will be copilots who are beginning their employment with an airline. Following the suggestions in Table 3, you contact students, institutional representatives, and professionals as well as identify a relevant paper on discrepancy reports.

After gathering some third-party information on discrepancy reports, you familiarize yourself with their characteristic lexical items and grammatical features by analyzing them in naturally occurring texts. Two features stand out as a result of your analysis: the reduced size of discrepancy reports and their formulaic structure (see Table 4).

Table 4. Patterned Language Use in Discrepancy Reports

Location	Part	Location	Discrepancy	Location	Extra info
Lower skin of	exhaust gate		corroded	at OTBD edge	
LT	floor support	at FRM 29-35	corroded		beyond limits
RT	horizontal angle		corroded		beyond limits

There are three compulsory elements in discrepancy reports: what the damaged part is, where it is located, and what the issue is. Location appears in different parts of the reports and can even feature more than once in a single report. Extra information about the problem can be included in discrepancy reports, but it is not an obligatory element.

Table 5 illustrates a simple way of recording—in an orderly manner—the information gathered from needs analysis. Once the needs analysis is done, it is important to decide whether there are suitable existing materials or new materials need to be developed (Bocanegra-Valle, 2010). In either case, the information collected through needs analysis should be used to inform the process.

Table 5. Data Collected From Needs Analysis for a Preservice ESP Course for Copilots

Course name: Writing Discrepancy Reports

Students' profile: Young adults (23–30 years old); Brazilians; 90% male; most of them studied at private schools; all of them are copilots with little flying experience (average of 200 flying hours) who have never flown wide-body planes; intermediate level of general English (B1–B2 in the Common European Framework of Reference for Languages); little knowledge of aviation English

Type of course: Preservice

Information—source	Skills	Genre	Vocabulary	Grammar	Tasks	Observed difficulties
Domain— professional context It was impossible to observe the relevant professional context.	—	—	—	—	—	—
Stakeholders— students Informal conversations and interviews were held.	Students do not know much about the genre, but they are interested and motivated to learn.					
Stakeholders— teachers and applied linguists No other person who had taught a similar course was contactable.	—	—	—	—	—	—

continued on next page

Table 5. *(continued)*

Information—source	Skills	Genre	Vocabulary	Grammar	Tasks	Observed difficulties
Stakeholders— institutions Informal conversations were held with an airline company chief pilot.	Writing	Discrepancy report	Parts of an aircraft, location words, nouns and verbs identifying problems (discrepancies)	—	Write a discrepancy report	Very little time to write the report
Stakeholders— professionals Informal conversations were held with experienced pilots.						Difficulty in remembering the names of the problems (discrepancies) in English and in understanding the acronyms used in the reports
Available literature— ESP materials and publications No suitable ESP materials were available, but a paper on this genre could be found: Farret (2012).			Frequently used parts of aircraft, location words, problems and acronyms	Passive voice, auxiliary verbs		Drury (2002 cited in Farret, 2012, p. 77) states that, with ever shorter times to perform external maintenance or inspection, pilots and mechanics find themselves challenged to work faster. This results in them performing these activities with less precision.
Target language— examples of texts Sample texts were observed. A small corpus was compiled and analyzed.			Parts of the aircraft, location words, nouns and verbs identifying problems (discrepancies)		—	—

CHAPTER 3

Genre

The results of your needs analysis are likely to indicate which genres should be targeted in the ESP course that you are designing (e.g., discrepancy reports in Table 5). This chapter starts by defining the concept of genre and relating it to the contexts in which ESP teachers may work. Attention is then given to how genre analysis can be undertaken and how to implement the genre-based approach in ESP courses.

REFLECTIVE QUESTIONS

Think of all the different moments in which you used language today.

- Who did you speak/write to?

- What did you read/listen to?

- For what purpose(s)?

Your answers to the reflection questions above probably included activities like reading the newspaper to be informed of current events, responding to an e-mail written by a student who missed the last test, and talking on the phone to make an appointment with the dentist. Each of these activities builds on our knowledge of genres, requiring us to use language in specific ways.

Definition of Genre

Genres are social practices that involve the use of language. They are materialized in texts that we encounter—either productively or receptively—in everyday life (e.g., note, phone call, menu, recipe, letter). All of our communication takes place through genres, including specialized communicative events. This is why ESP teachers should have at least a basic understanding of genres and know how to analyze them.

A genre is "a recognizable communicative event characterized by a set of communicative purpose(s) identified and mutually understood by the members of the professional or academic community in which it regularly occurs" (Bhatia, 1993, p. 13). Communicative purpose, the most important factor in the identification of genres (Bhatia, 1993; Swales, 1990), refers to the reasons for interacting—in other words, why people use language. For example, the main communicative purpose of a tourism brochure is to convince readers to visit the attraction(s) featured in the brochure.

In addition to communicative purpose, other relevant factors include content, intended audience, form, and channel. For instance, the content of business meetings can include sales of a product (e.g., car) or service (e.g., banking applications). These meetings can be attended by the senior management personnel at a company, who will have decision-making powers, or by collaborators, who will listen to the offer and then report it to their line managers. The meetings can be informal (e.g., two parties will sit and talk about the offer) or may involve a prepared formal presentation. They can be conducted in a number of channels such as in person, by teleconference or video conference, or online.

Genres are "relatively stable types" (Bakhtin, 1986, p. 60), and we recognize them on the basis of our previous experiences. Although each new text has some degree of creativity, some textual characteristics are routinely repeated in specific written/spoken texts. The stability of genres

Teaching English for Specific Purposes

and their recurrent nature in our lives allow us to recognize whether a text is a recipe, for example. A bloody mary recipe is different from a martini recipe, but everyone would be able to tell they are both recipes—and not oven user manuals.

> **REFLECTIVE QUESTION**
>
> - Considering the ESP course you are teaching (or planning to teach), which genres would be most relevant for your students to learn?

Relationship Between Genres and Discourse Communities

An important concept in the identification of genres is discourse communities (Swales, 1990), that is, groups in which individuals identify with one another through, for instance, occupational factors like journalism or engineering. These communities share a particular repertoire of genres. For example, doctors use medical charts to keep a record of diagnoses, test results, prescribed drugs, and so on. The charts help to avoid miscommunication among doctors and nurses during changes of shift so that patients continue to have appropriate care.

Genres, however, are not tied to only one specific discourse community. They can circulate within one or more discourse communities. For example, written prescriptions, which are produced by doctors, are aimed at allowing patients to purchase their prescribed drugs from pharmacists. Thus, pharmacists have to understand the prescription accurately so that they can provide patients with the correct medicine.

Using genres effectively shows professionals' ability to participate in the discourse community(ies) to which they belong. Thus, when we consider ESP courses, it is important to know the genres that the relevant discourse community uses and whether students will need to consume (i.e., listen, read) and/or produce (i.e., speak, write) them. Table 6 relates specific fields to potentially relevant genres to be included in ESP courses.

Table 6. Potential Genres to Be Learned by Two Different ESP Student Cohorts

Professionals	Genres	Skills	Interactants	Purposes
Bartenders	Orders	Speaking and listening	Customers	Request drinks to be served
	Recipes	Reading	Recipe writer	Explain how drinks should be made
	Small talk	Speaking and listening	Customers	Greet and entertain customers
	Code of conduct	Reading	Managers	Outline responsibilities and expected work practices
Commercial Pilots	Radiotelephony	Listening and speaking	Air traffic controllers	Exchange information about the flow of air traffic in a specific region/airport
	Operations manuals	Reading	Aircraft manufacturers	Explain how a specific airplane works
	Discrepancy reports	Writing	Mechanics	Report on aircraft problems
	Automatic terminal information service recordings	Listening	Automated text-to-speech recordings (only in very small airports are these recordings undertaken by humans)	Inform pilots about the current weather, active runways, available approaches, and other needed information

Table 6 indicates that two student cohorts—bartenders and commercial pilots—require knowledge of different genres to succeed in their jobs. In an ESP course for bartenders, it would make no sense to teach discrepancy reports because these professionals do not have to use such a genre in their professional practice. These two groups belong to different discourse communities and, hence, communicate through different genres.

Not only does Table 6 indicate genres that are potentially relevant to two student groups, but it also highlights what kind of engagement (i.e., productive or receptive) is required in each case. While operations manuals are relevant to commercial pilots, these professionals only need to read the manuals. There is little point in teaching operations manual writing because pilots will not have to fulfill this duty outside the classroom.

Genre Analysis for ESP Teachers

Genre analysis is important for ESP teachers since it enhances their understanding of the main contextual and linguistic features of the different specialized texts that they will have to teach. In order to understand genres, it is important to identify who speaks/writes, with/to whom, for what purpose, in what situation, where, in what way, through what support, and in what format. This knowledge of (often unfamiliar) specialized genres is key in ensuring that ESP teachers design appropriate tasks for their students.

Bhatia (1993) uses a printed sales letter to illustrate genre analysis. He singles out three main communicative features of this genre:

- The addressees are prospective customers who may come to purchase a specific product or service.

- This is an example of an unsolicited genre—the addressees have not requested the letter and most of them are unlikely to be interested in the advertised product or service (i.e., it is difficult to persuade addressees to take action).

- As the letter is aimed at "initiating business relations," it should "encourage further communication between the two parties" (p. 46).

In addition to identifying the general characteristics of the genre, Bhatia (1993) specifies and illustrates its moves, that is, the sections that fulfill different communicative purposes (Ding, 2007). In the case of the printed sales letter genre, Bhatia proposes seven moves:

1. establishing credentials
2. introducing the offer
3. offering incentives
4. enclosing documents
5. soliciting response
6. using pressure tactics
7. ending politely (p. 48)

The penultimate move—using pressure tactics—is exemplified in this excerpt: "As the number of participants at each training programme is limited, we would urge you to finalize as soon as possible your plans to participate" (Bhatia, 1993, p. 48).

REFLECTIVE QUESTION

- Think of a genre you usually work with in class. What are its main moves?

Genre-Based Approach in ESP Courses

While it is extremely useful for ESP teachers to understand the genres that they will have to teach, the genre analysis detailed above may be difficult for ESP students and, hence, time-consuming to be carried out in class. However, raising ESP students' genre awareness does not necessarily require much class time. The following questions could be used to trigger students' guided discovery about the genres with which they will need to engage in their professions.

- Who produces the genre? (i.e., Who is the addressor?)
- Who consumes it? (i.e., Who is the addressee?)
- What is (are) its main move(s)?

- Which features help you identify this text as an example of the given genre? (e.g., How can you tell a letter is a letter and not a recipe?)

- What role do you and/or the discourse community to which you belong play in relation to this genre? (i.e., Are you the addressor or the addressee?)

- Which skill(s) do you need in your interaction with this genre (i.e., reading, writing, speaking, listening)?

Depending on your students' prior knowledge, you could ask them to analyze the genre themselves (see, e.g., Table 4), or you could ask students to match moves with specific fragments of the genre.

Flowerdew (2000) proposes some activities to raise students' awareness of the specificities of academic writing, some of which would be suitable to ESP students:

- Reconstructing a text: Teachers cut out the text into parts and ask students to put them together in the correct order.

- Comparing texts: Teachers show a number of examples of the same genre and ask students to check whether they all fulfill the same specific purposes, have similar structures, and so on.

Students should then be asked to identify typical linguistic features in the genre that they are studying. The following two chapters, which deal with specialized vocabulary and corpus linguistics, offer ideas of how to conduct more detailed linguistic analyses of different specialized genres and how these analyses may inform ESP teaching.

CHAPTER 4

Specialized Vocabulary

This chapter deals with specialized vocabulary, an important language system in the understanding of genres in ESP. Following a brief conceptual discussion, the chapter focuses on the vocabulary needs of ESP learners and the ways in which ESP teachers can deal with this specialized vocabulary in the classroom. The chapter also provides useful suggestions on how students can decipher long terminological units and develop autonomous vocabulary learning strategies.

Specialized Vocabulary in ESP

When words and multiword units have a specific meaning in one area of specialism, they are called terms (e.g., *stair, clamp, lever, spring*) or terminological units (e.g., *dual-circuit outside brake, two independently acting brake blocks*). These units are usually nouns or noun phrases, but verbs or verb phrases can also convey terminological meaning (e.g., *pivot the rope guard, bolt the rope guard*).

Terms and terminological units can collectively be referred to as terminology, specialized vocabulary, special purpose vocabulary, or technical vocabulary. Whether this specialized vocabulary is the main focus of ESP classes depends on the tasks performed by ESP students in their professional domain, their objectives when performing these tasks, and the amount of specialized knowledge they have. As Cabré and Estopá (2003, p. 217) put it,

> Different professional groups do not only have different terminological needs as a result of the tasks they perform, but their training needs are also conditioned by their objectives and level of knowledge of specialised themes and professional language, as well as by those needs pertaining to the relevant types of units.

All this information should be collected during the process of needs analysis (see Chapter 2).

ESP Learners' Vocabulary Needs

REFLECTIVE QUESTIONS

- Which vocabulary do (will) you teach in your ESP classes?
- What evidence from your needs analysis supports your decision?

The most appropriate answer to the question that opens this section is "It depends." It depends on your ESP learners' profiles and backgrounds (e.g., age, nationality, professional experience, proficiency level, educational background), the professional knowledge that they already have, their perceived lexical needs to perform their jobs successfully in English, and the genres that they need to master (see Chapter 3), to mention just a few. That is why no ESP course should be designed without a thorough and systematic needs analysis (see Chapter 2).

The remainder of this section considers the planning of an in-service ESP course for a group of novice technicians who are fluent in general English and whose first language is Spanish. They have just started working for a company that manufactures elevators. To perform their assigned duties adequately, the technicians are expected to read and understand texts from manuals written in English like the one reproduced in Figure 3.

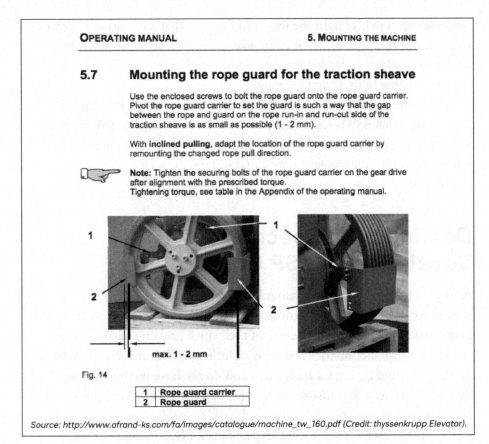

Source: http://www.afrand-ks.com/fa/images/catalogue/machine_tw_160.pdf (Credit: thyssenkrupp Elevator).

Figure 3. Excerpt From an Elevator Operating Manual

REFLECTIVE QUESTION

- Considering the student profile outlined above, which words or multiword units from the text in Figure 3 would you teach?

Showing learners what they already know in a specialized text is usually an encouraging and motivating way of starting a vocabulary class. Given the Romance language background of the target student group, it is possible to imagine that they would have some advantage (compared to learners from other first language backgrounds) in their reading of the manual in Figure 3. Petrescu, Helms-Park, and Dronjic (2017) point out that "in highly specialized disciplines, speakers' language backgrounds would impact the ease or difficulty of acquiring discipline-specific terminology" (p. 15). Asking these target learners to highlight the words in Figure 3 that have either Greek or Latin origin (e.g., *operating, manual, use, guard, possible, inclined, adapt, location*) would draw their attention to the fact that many of these words are similar to those in their first language.

After the cognate words have been identified, what is left in the text is probably what ESP teachers have to focus in their classes: terms (e.g., *sheave, screw, gap, gear, drive*) and terminological units (e.g., *the rope run-in and run-out side, the changed rope pull direction, the securing bolts, the gear drive*).

Dealing With Specialized Vocabulary in ESP Courses

As our example ESP course is aimed at novice technicians who have just started working for a specific company, understanding the information presented in manuals might be one of their most pressing needs. Using general English dictionaries is usually of little help. Oftentimes specialized dictionaries and glossaries are limited and do not have the information that students need. Because terms and terminological units are the lexical elements that convey specialized knowledge in a professional domain, they should be the focus of the vocabulary lessons for this student cohort.

Images can be explored to help students understand specialized vocabulary. As Faber, Araúz, Prieto Velasco, and Reimerink (2006, p. 49) explain, "The inclusion of different types of visual representation is extremely helpful in specialized knowledge fields since images enhance textual comprehension and complement the linguistic information provided in other data fields." ESP teachers can ask questions about images and other visual elements before starting to work with the actual text to activate students' background knowledge and enhance students' textual comprehension. In Figure 3, for example, the ESP teacher could draw students' attention to the fact that there can be a distance of only 1 to 2 mm between two components. When reading the text, it would probably be easier for students to understand the excerpt of the manual, which explains this distance limitation: "The gap between the rope and guard on the rope run-in and run-out side of the traction sheave is as small as possible (1–2 mm)."

The co-text can also be used, as suggested by Pearson (2000), to support students' understanding of terms and terminological units. Some of the clues mentioned by Pearson are (a) phrases that usually provide information about purpose, inputs, outputs, and properties (e.g., *used for, used to, involve, produce*) and (b) expressions that indicate quasi-synonymous relations (e.g., *called, known as, i.e., e.g.*; p. 97). The manual excerpt in Figure 3 shows, for instance, use of the infinite to indicate purpose: "Use the enclosed screws *to bolt the rope guard onto the rope guard carrier*" (emphasis added).

REFLECTIVE QUESTION

- If you have taught or observed ESP classes, what problems did students experience in reading texts from their professional background? How did they overcome these problems?

Deciphering Long Terminological Units

A common problem ESP learners face when learning specialized vocabulary is deciphering long terminological units (e.g., *overhead door caution annunciator panel, aluminum and fiberglass honeycomb-core material, forward and aft electronic control panel lights brightness*). These units cannot usually be found in dictionaries or glossaries, restricting the sources that students can turn to in order to learn them.

In English, terminological units are generally made up of a head noun and modifiers. Modifiers usually come before the head noun, specifying its meaning. In *aluminum and fiberglass honeycomb-core material*, for example, the head noun *material* is modified by *aluminum, fiberglass,* and *honeycomb-core*. If students understand how each modifier specifies the meaning of the head noun, it will probably be easier for them to make sense of the terminological unit. In the example given, the *material* is made of *aluminum* and *fiberglass*. The hyphen in *honeycomb-core* indicates a submodification; that is, the *core* or the central part of the material is modified by *honeycomb*, which indicates its format. The modifiers in this terminological unit describe what the material consists of and how it is shaped.

Another strategy that might help students understand the meaning of terminological units is to teach them to start reading these expressions from the head noun and then moving to the left (e.g., *material* with a *honeycomb core*, which is made up of *aluminum* and *fiberglass*). In certain cases (especially when students have low English proficiency), it might also help to translate the units to their first language. In Spanish, *aluminum and fiberglass honeycomb-core material* would be *material con un núcleo de panal hecho de fibra de vidrio y aluminio.* It is important to show students that, with some terminological units, this strategy may not work or may not represent the meaning that the unit has in a specific domain. For example, the unit *center wing box* does not mean *caja de ala central* in Spanish, which would be the case if the suggested reading strategy were applied (i.e., one could have the impression that the unit referred to the box of the central wing, as if there were two other wings, like in a triplane). The context—the manual of a commercial aircraft—clarifies that *center wing box* actually means *the box in the central part of the wing*, which in Spanish would be *caja central del ala.*

Autonomous Vocabulary Learning Strategies

As ESP teachers, we do not need to be specialists in the areas that we teach, which means that we are not always aware of terminological meaning. We should work together with students and look for strategies that can be used to solve their terminological questions. One activity is to ask students to bring to class a text that they might have to read in their professional practice. In class, students should be asked to underline five terms or terminological units that they do not know. Afterward, students should be encouraged to discover the meaning of their underlined terms/terminological units without the teacher's help. The Internet can be a useful source in this regard as students may be able to find the information they need online autonomously. This section presents some simple strategies that can be used by ESP students.

Definitions

A very simple strategy that can be used when you want some information about a word is to type "define:*x*" in Google's search box, where *x* stands for the word to be defined. However, using this strategy with terms and terminological units does not always produce good results.

Academic Definitions

Using Google Scholar, you can search for terms or terminological units in academic outputs. If you want to look up a specific phrase such as *grassroots diplomacy*, it is just a matter of searching for this phrase within quotation marks. To try to find a definition, you can add verbs like *be*, *define*, and *mean* in the search string (e.g., *is*, *can be defined as*, *means*). Using this strategy with "grassroots diplomacy is," it is possible to retrieve definitions like "grassroots diplomacy is the art of understanding this multiplicity and complexity of worldviews and cultural frameworks and resolving conflict in the best interest of the stakeholders and the venture" (Mehta & Dzombak, 2013, p. 208), which may help clarify the meaning of this phrase.

Translations and Equivalents in Another Language

Resources like Google Translate (https://translate.google.com) and InterActive Terminology for Europe (IATE; http://iate.europa.eu) can be used to find translations and equivalents in another language.

Figure 4 shows an adequate equivalent in Spanish for *data breaches* provided by Google Translate.

Figure 4. Google Translate's Spanish Equivalent for Data Breach

However, Google Translate may not be the best option when it comes to finding equivalents of terms in specialized contexts. It tells us that the Spanish equivalent for *stakeholder* is *tenedor de apuestas* (see Figure 5), which is not an appropriate equivalent for the term in the field of international relations.

Figure 5. Google Translate's Spanish Equivalent for Stakeholder

In this case, a better option would be to use IATE, which offers the possibility of finding equivalents from a wide variety of source and target languages as well as in different domains (see Figure 6).

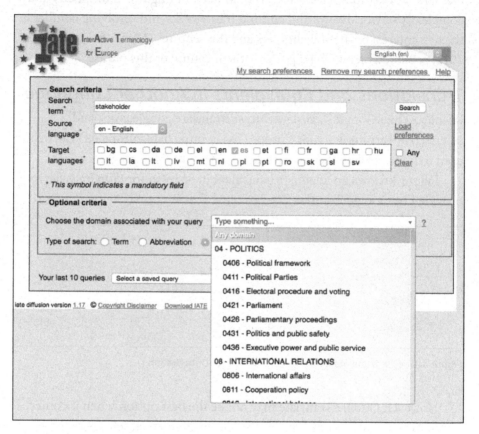

Figure 6. IATE's Search Interface

Figure 7 shows three equivalents of *stakeholder* in Spanish: *interesado*, *parte interesada*, and *parte implicada*.

Teaching English for Specific Purposes

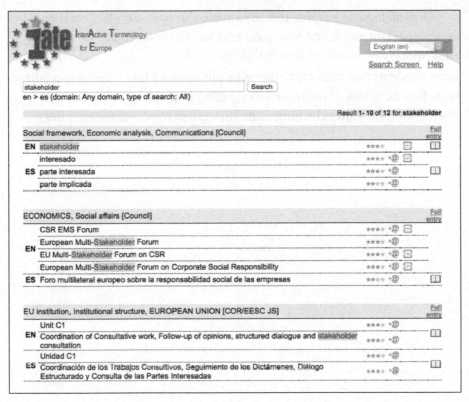

Figure 7. *IATE's Spanish Equivalents for* Stakeholder

Once an equivalent is found, the earlier strategies related to definitions and academic definitions can be used to find these kinds of definitions in the learner's first language.

Images

Finally, in some specialized contexts, seeing an image is enough for the student to understand the meaning of the unknown term or terminological unit. Image search engines (e.g., Google Images, Yahoo Images) and specialized sites (e.g., Biodigital, www.biodigital.com; UCSB Bisque system, http://bioimage.ucsb.edu/bisque) can be used for this purpose. For instance, a Google Images search for *aluminum and fiberglass honeycomb-core material* would easily show students what material is being alluded to.

As ESP teachers, we must strive to develop our students' autonomy, and the Internet can be used in this regard. We must also remind our students of the need to triangulate the information they find online to ensure its validity and reliability.

Organizing and keeping this information in open-access glossaries is very important and might be a good idea for a course project. By creating these glossaries, students will exercise their mining strategies as well as help other students that might face the same difficulties while reading specialized texts (see *LÚMINA Idiomas* for an example of a glossary in English and Portuguese, www.ufrgs.br/luminaidiomas/index.php?r=glossary/index).

CHAPTER 5

Corpus Linguistics

The previous chapter focused on specialized vocabulary, which generally presents challenges to ESP teachers who may have little to no knowledge of their students' specialism. When we are asked to teach an ESP course, the results of our needs analysis will be instrumental in helping us decide what to teach. However, we may find it challenging to identify what language items to teach in our courses, especially if few ESP materials are available on the market or if they do not cater for our students' needs. One way of overcoming this issue is to draw on corpus linguistics. The following sections detail how we can work with general, specialized, and custom-made collections of text.

REFLECTION QUESTIONS

- What (if anything) do you know about corpus linguistics?

- Which corpora have you heard of? What do you know about them?

Definition of Corpus Linguistics

A corpus (plural form: corpora) is "a collection of (1) machine readable (2) authentic texts (including transcripts of spoken data) which is (3) sampled to be (4) representative of a particular language or particular variety" (McEnery, Xiao, & Tono, 2006, p. 5; see also Viana, Zyngier, & Barnbrook, 2011). Corpora comprise naturally occurring language; the texts included in these collections have been produced by real speakers and writers for specific communicative goals.

As its name indicates, corpus linguistics (CL) makes use of corpora in language research. It sees language as a probabilistic system: Although many combinations and linguistic features are possible, they are not all likely to occur. For example, while adjectives can precede nouns in English, CL focuses on the likelihood of a specific adjective (e.g., *blue, white, yellow*) being used before a given noun (e.g., *sky*). CL has considerably advanced our knowledge of word patterns and drawn attention to the importance of teaching word combinations and sequences—rather than isolated words.

Main Types of Corpora

There are two main types of corpora: general and specialized. A general corpus is representative of a language as a whole and can be used to investigate patterns that are pervasive in that specific language. This corpus usually has different spoken and written genres (e.g., news stories, face-to-face conversations). An example is the British National Corpus (BNC; https://corpus.byu.edu/bnc/), a 100-million-word corpus created to represent British English mostly from the 1980s. On the other hand, a specialized corpus concentrates on a specific use of a language, such as a particular subject area (business English) or genre (discrepancy reports written by commercial pilots). The Hong Kong Corpus of Surveying and Construction Engineering (HKCSCE; http://rcpce.engl.polyu.edu.hk/HKCSCE/) is an example of a specialized corpus; it contains texts from six genres (e.g., media releases, reports) in the engineering specialism.

Using General Corpora

Corpora can be used by the two main stakeholders in ESP courses: teachers and students. We teachers can use corpora to learn (more) about the language that we have to teach, write syllabi, and design pedagogical materials, among other uses. Students can use corpora to solve their language problems—as if they were language detectives, an approach known as data-driven learning (T. Johns, 1990; see also Viana, 2010, 2015, in press, for practical classroom applications).

There are several general corpora available online that ESP teachers and students can freely consult. One example is the Corpus of Contemporary American English (COCA; https://corpus.byu.edu/coca), which has over 560 million words. The texts in the COCA are classified into five sections (spoken, fiction, magazine, newspaper, and academic) and several subsections. As ESP teachers, we may find it more useful to access just part of this corpus. For example, if you were to teach an ESP course to sports journalists, you could find appropriate material in the sports subsection within news.

In the COCA, one can easily examine the frequencies of words as well as their patterns. A much-needed word in the sports field is *goal* since it is a way of scoring points in a number of sports (e.g., American football, hockey, soccer). It is therefore likely that journalists will have to use it in the news stories that they write. To investigate its co-text in the COCA (see Figure 8), we would need to (1) click on the "Search" tab at the top of the screen (this is generally already selected by default when you visit the site for the first time), (2) type *goal* in the search box, (3) click on "Sections" for the corresponding menu to appear, (4) choose the appropriate section (in this case, "NEWS:Sports"), and (5) click on "Find matching strings."

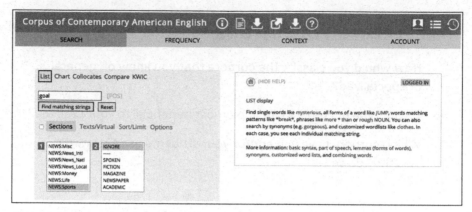

Figure 8. Search Interface (List) in the COCA

At the time of writing, the search returns 3,277 occurrences of *goal* (see Figure 9). This total may change as the COCA evolves over time with the inclusion of new texts.

SEE CONTEXT: CLICK ON WORD OR SELECT WORDS + [CONTEXT] [HELP...]				COMPARE
	■	CONTEXT	FREQ	
1	▣	GOAL	3277	
				0.734 seconds

Figure 9. Results for Goal in the COCA NEWS:Sports Section

This quantitative result does not tell anything about how *goal* is actually used in sports news stories. We should therefore examine its patterning, following Firth's (1957, p. 11) famous quote: "You shall know a word by the company it keeps." By clicking on the word *goal* in Figure 9, we have access to its co-text as well as to the year and source of the publications (see Figure 10).

A first glance at Figure 10 reveals that *goal* can mean a successful scoring attempt (Lines 1, 2, 8, 17), the area where the ball or puck must be thrown or hit to score a point (Lines 5, 6, 14), or an aim (Lines 3, 7, 9–13, 15, 16, 18–20). Considering that our example ESP course is for sports journalists, we would be interested in the two first specialized meanings.

We can learn more about the word *goal* by using the Collocates functionality in the COCA, which enables us to see the words that go together, providing useful insights into meaning and usage. To do so, we would click on (1) "Collocates" (on the "Search" page), (2) the number 4 on the left and on the right, and (3) "Find collocates" (see Figure 11; note that the asterisk appears by default when we do not specify a word or word class in the search field next to "Collocates").

Teaching English for Specific Purposes

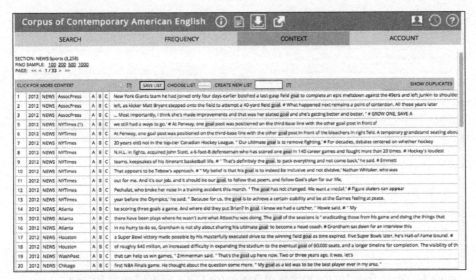

Figure 10. Examples of Goal in the COCA NEWS:Sports Section

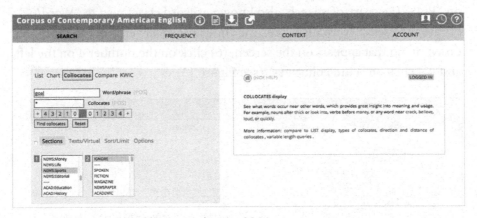

Figure 11. Search Interface (Collocates) in the COCA

Searching for all the words that precede and follow *goal* (up to a maximum of four on each side) in newspaper sports texts returns the results shown in Figure 12. We can see that *field* is the most frequently occurring word in the co-text of *goal*, totaling 1,226 joint occurrences. Most of the times these words appear in the multiword unit *field goal* from American football and basketball. The second most frequent company is *scored*, which is a lexical verb used to say a player was successful in his or her attempt at a goal.

Our group of ESP journalists is likely to write stories reporting on goals, so they may benefit from learning which lexical verbs are used with *goal*. To do so in the COCA, we would (1) click on the "Search" tab, (2) click on "Collocates," (3) type *goal* in the "Word/phrase" search box, (4) click

		CONTEXT	FREQ	ALL	%	MI	
1	☐	FIELD	1226	10563	11.61	5.96	▬▬▬▬▬▬▬▬
2	☐	SCORED	153	6436	2.38	3.67	▬▬
3	☐	LINE	148	7376	2.01	3.42	▬▬
4	☐	KICKED	102	576	17.71	6.57	▬
5	☐	PERCENTAGE	97	1165	8.33	5.48	▬
6	☐	SECONDS	86	2609	3.30	4.14	▬
7	☐	MISSED	72	2967	2.43	3.70	▬
8	☐	ATTEMPT	47	858	5.48	4.87	▪
9	☐	OVERTIME	47	1236	3.80	4.35	▪
10	☐	GAME-WINNING	45	348	12.93	6.11	▪
11	☐	BLOCKED	42	749	5.61	4.91	▪
12	☐	ATTEMPTS	40	632	6.33	5.08	▪
13	☐	ULTIMATE	36	368	9.78	5.71	▪
14	☐	SCORER	32	817	3.92	4.39	▪
15	☐	TYING	30	413	7.26	5.28	▪
16	☐	2ND	26	580	4.48	4.58	▪
17	☐	ASSIST	21	229	9.17	5.62	▪
18	☐	32-YARD	20	48	41.67	7.80	▪
19	☐	MAIN	20	974	2.05	3.46	▪
20	☐	28-YARD	19	59	32.20	7.43	▪

Figure 12. Words Found in the Vicinity of Goal *in the COCA NEWS:Sports Section*

on "POS" (i.e., part-of-speech, also known as word class) next to "Word/ phrase," (5) select "verb.LEX" (i.e., the code for lexical verb) in the drop-down menu that appears on the screen, (6) click on the number 4 on the left, and (7) click on "Find collocates" (see Figure 13).

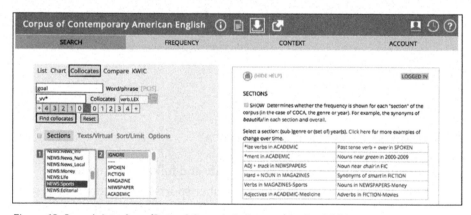

Figure 13. Search Interface (Part-of-Speech Collocates) in the COCA

Figure 14 shows the results for the lexical verbs found to the left (maximum of four words) of *goal*. S*core* is the most common lexical verb used with *goal* and, as expected, it is most frequently used in the past, totaling 139 hits. The results additionally reveal a number of other combinations with verbs such as *kick, set, get, miss,* and *make.* The next step would be to examine their respective concordance lines (cf. Figure 10) to study the use of these combinations of lexical verbs with *goal* more closely.

Teaching English for Specific Purposes

		CONTEXT	FREQ	
1	☐	SCORED	139	
2	☐	KICKED	99	
3	☐	SET	38	
4	☐	GOT	37	
5	☐	MISSED	33	
6	☐	SAID	32	
7	☐	MADE	24	
8	☐	KICK	21	
9	☐	SCORING	21	
10	☐	SCORE	20	
11	☐	ADDED	16	
12	☐	ACHIEVE	14	
13	☐	BLOCKED	12	
14	☐	ALLOWED	11	
15	☐	REACH	11	
16	☐	SETTLE	11	
17	☐	REACHED	10	
18	☐	CROSSED	9	
19	☐	ACCOMPLISH	9	
20	☐	HIT	9	

Figure 14. Lexical Verbs That Precede Goal *in the COCA NEWS:Sports Section*

REFLECTION QUESTIONS

- What lexical verbs do you think are most commonly used with *point*?

- How does your answer differ from the empirical results you arrive at after analyzing the COCA data? (Repeat the procedures described in this section for the word *point*.)

- Check the other COCA functionalities. Do you think they are useful for your students? How so?

Using Specialized Corpora

In addition to general corpora, we can also take advantage of specialized corpora in our ESP practice. The Research Centre for Professional Communication in English (RCPCE; http://rcpce.engl.polyu.edu.hk/index .html) at Hong Kong Polytechnic University, for example, offers a variety of profession-specific corpora such as the Hong Kong Corpus of Surveying and Construction Engineering (HKCSCE) and the Hong Kong Financial Services Corpus (HKFSC). The latter is a 7.3-million-word collection of texts from the financial sector from 25 genres (e.g., annual reports, media releases, prospectuses).

The search function in the HKFSC will be intuitive to those who are familiar with the COCA interface, despite their differences (see Figure 15).

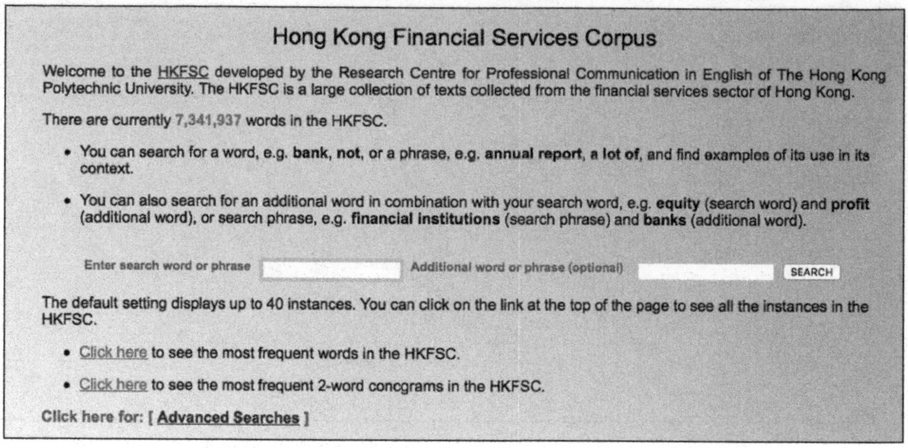

Figure 15. Search Interface in the HKFSC

The HKFSC provides two frequency lists: the 200 most frequent words and the 200 most frequent two-word combinations ("concgrams" in Figure 15). This information is important because frequency can be a criterion to be used in selecting items to be taught in an ESP course.

The top 25 two-word combinations (regardless of their internal order) in the HKFSC can be found online (http://rcpce.engl.polyu.edu.hk/HKFSC /CG2_A-Z_EXCL_cutoff10.htm). Some of the most frequent combinations are *cent+per*, *company+limited*, *as+such*, and *exchange+stock*.

To find out how *exchange+stock* is used, that is, to learn about its co-text, simply type the phrase in the "Enter search word or phrase" field and click on "Search" (see Figure 15). As expected, *exchange stock* yields a limited number of occurrences (only two). However, *stock exchange* is more frequently used; it totals 3,634 instances.

As a follow-up activity, we could ask students, for instance, to find out which preposition precedes *the stock exchange* (e.g., *at, in, on*) and study their respective co-texts. Given the HKFSC interface, the exact phrases would need to be searched for individually (e.g., *at the stock market, in the stock market, on the stock market*). The results show

- no instances of *at the stock exchange*;

- 27 instances of *in the stock exchange*—in 20 of them, *stock exchange* modifies *daily quotations* (e.g., "(i) the closing price of the share as stated in the Stock Exchange's daily quotations sheet on the date of grant, which must be a dealing day");

Teaching English for Specific Purposes

- 653 instances of *on the stock exchange* in which reference is made to the actual place/bourse where stock brokers and traders can buy and sell shares of stock, bonds, and other securities (e.g., "An option can be exercised in whole or in part provided it is exercised in respect of a board lot for dealing in shares on the Stock Exchange or an integral multiples thereof").

Working With Custom-Made Corpora

In several ESP scenarios, teachers might need to create their own corpora. For instance, it would probably be difficult to find a corpus of discrepancy reports to support the development of materials for a preservice ESP course for copilots (see Chapter 2). Such a corpus would contain discrepancy reports written by different professionals on a variety of problems. You may be able to find texts for your specialized corpus in specific websites and/or you can rely on your students to provide you with these texts. The texts in a corpus are usually stored separately in plain text format (i.e., those generated in Notepad in Windows with the extension .TXT) and then uploaded into specific software (e.g., AntConc, www.laurenceanthony.net/software /antconc/; WordSmith Tools, http://lexically.net/wordsmith/).

Sarmento (2008) used corpus tools to investigate three ESP-relevant manuals: an operations manual and a quick reference handbook written for pilots and a maintenance manual (MM) produced for mechanics. Here we focus on the latter, which contained 249,691 words.

The literature on aviation technical manuals indicates frequent use of modal verbs to express obligations, possibilities, and consequences (Shawcross, 1992). For this reason, Sarmento (2008) researched the nine central modal verbs in English in the MM. The results showed that, while *might* and *would* are nearly absent from the MM, *can*, *must*, and *will* are frequently used (Sarmento, 2008, p. 158).

The next step was to examine how these modal verbs were used in the text. After a manual analysis of all the occurrences of *can* in the MM, Sarmento (2008) noticed that this modal verb

- is used mostly in affirmative sentences, which are 10 times more frequent than negative ones;
- is more frequently found in the active voice, and around 30% of these active voice occurrences have *you* as the subject;

- expresses possibility in most cases;

- is frequently found in the WARNING or CAUTION sections (written in capital letters), where *can* is always followed by a verb expressing negative meanings such as *damage* and *cause*.

Translating Corpus Findings Into ESP Pedagogy

Sarmento's (2008) analysis informed the development of a 120-hour ESP course for aviation mechanics and technicians who had only basic knowledge of English and who needed to read maintenance manuals in detail. Being able to understand just the gist of these manuals would not suffice because the instructions needed to be strictly followed. This way, the language to be taught had to be carefully chosen.

We believe that frequency of words and multiword units in corpora should be one of the criteria (although not the only one) to inform decisions about what to teach in ESP courses. Considering the findings presented in the previous section, this means that the ESP course for aviation mechanics and technicians should focus primarily on the most frequent modal verbs: *can*, *will*, *must*, and *may*. The other modal verbs would receive reduced attention in class, with *might* and *would* being virtually absent.

Corpus exploration has the added benefit of providing plenty of examples of language in use. We hold that this is a must in ESP to allow (future) professionals to be introduced to and become familiar with the language they will have to understand in their day-to-day tasks. In the case of the ESP course for aviation mechanics and technicians, the language used in the pedagogical materials deviated from contrived examples made up by the teacher. Instead, it privileged sentences extracted from the manual where modal verbs had been used.

REFLECTION QUESTIONS

- How useful do you think corpus linguistics is to your practice?

- What specialized corpora would be most appropriate to you and your students?

- What would you search for in these corpora?

CHAPTER 6

Conclusion

In line with the aims of this book series, the previous chapters provided an overview of four topics within ESP: needs analysis, genre, specialized vocabulary, and corpus linguistics. Each of these topics could have received a book-length treatment, as in Brown (2016) with regard to needs analysis and Hyon (2018) in relation to genre. Numerous other topics such as course design (e.g., Woodrow, 2018) could have been discussed here as well. Our approach was to introduce you to some of the main concepts, show how these may be applied to teaching ESP, and invite you to reflect on their relevance to your classroom context. We would like to stress this last point: You are the insider when it comes to your work environment, so you should be in charge of deciding what is (un)feasible to implement. Throughout the book, we have included questions to guide your reflection on the applicability of the concepts reviewed and the suggestions given.

Next Steps

There is considerable ground to be explored in our field. As Holliday (1994, p. 9) writes, "A great deal of research has been done in all aspects of English language education, and yet there are still significant gaps in our knowledge which prevent us from achieving classroom methodologies appropriate for different situations." One could see this from a negative or a positive standpoint. We prefer to stick to the latter option: The fact that there is so much to be examined is truly exciting. We can engage ourselves in this exploration and contribute to our field.

If you are planning to add to the research knowledge in ESP, it is worthwhile checking *English for Specific Purposes* (www.journals.elsevier .com/english-for-specific-purposes/), the main journal in the field. Browsing its contents allows you to see the current topics in ESP and what areas can be explored. Unfortunately, however, the journal is not open-access, so it might not be available to colleagues whose institutions do not subscribe to it. Other relevant publications include the following:

- *Asian ESP Journal* (www.asian-esp-journal.com/)

- *ASp* (http://journals.openedition.org/asp/?lang=en), originally in French

- *ESP World* (www.esp-world.info/)

- *IATEFL ESP SIG Journal* (https://espsig.iatefl.org)

- *Ibérica* (www.aelfe.org/?s=presentacio), originally in Spanish

- *The ESPecialist* (https://revistas.pucsp.br/esp), originally in Portuguese

Your contributions do not necessarily need to be research-driven and wide-encompassing, though. You can engage in small-scale, reflective investigations about your own context. This type of research is extremely useful in ensuring better learning experiences for your students.

Whatever path you decide to take, we very much encourage you to (continue to) engage in ESP professional development in the years to come.

REFLECTIVE QUESTIONS

- What project can you undertake to improve your ESP teaching skills?

- Which topic (whether or not discussed in this volume) would you like to learn more about? What will you do to achieve this goal?

References

Bakhtin, M. (1986). *Speech genres and other late essays* (V. W. McGee, Trans.). Austin: University of Texas Press.

Bhatia, V. (1993). *Analysing genre: Language use in professional settings*. London, England: Longman.

Bocanegra-Valle, A. (2010). Evaluating and designing materials for the ESP classroom. In M. F. Ruiz-Garrido, J. C. Palmer-Silveira, & I. Fortanet Gomez (Eds.), *English for professional and academic purposes* (pp. 141–165). Amsterdam, Netherlands: Rodopi.

Brown, J. D. (2016). *Introducing needs analysis and English for specific purposes*. Abingdon, England: Routledge.

Cabré, M. T., & Estopá, R. (2003). On the units of specialized meaning used in professional communication. *Terminology Science and Research, 1*, 217–237.

Ding, H. (2007). Genre analysis of personal statements: Analysis of moves in application essays to medical and dental schools. *English for Specific Purposes, 26*, 368–392.

Dudley-Evans, T. (2001). English for specific purposes. In R. Carter & D. Nunan (Eds.), *The Cambridge guide to teaching English to speakers of other languages* (pp. 131–136). Cambridge, England: Cambridge University Press.

Faber, P., Araúz, P. L., Prieto Velasco, J. A., & Reimerink, A. (2006). Linking images and words: the description of specialized concepts. *International Journal of Lexicography, 20*(1), 39–65.

Farret, L. F. (2012). Reporte de itens de discrepância na aviação civil: Um estudo baseado em um corpus especializado [Discrepancy item reports in civil aviation: A study based on a specialized corpus]. *Aviation in Focus—Journal of Aeronautical Sciences, 3*(2), 76–90. Retrieved from http://revistaseletronicas.pucrs.br/ojs/index.php /aviation

Firth, J. R. (1957). *Papers in linguistics: 1934–1951*. London, England: Oxford University Press.

Flowerdew, L. (2000). Using a genre-based framework to teach organizational structure in academic writing. *ELT Journal, 54*, 369–378.

Flowerdew, L. (2013). Needs analysis and curriculum development in ESP. In B. Paltridge & S. Starfield (Eds.), *The handbook of English for specific purposes* (pp. 325–346). Chichester, England: Wiley Blackwell.

Gomm, H., & Hird, J. (2001). *Inside out advanced: Teacher's book*. Oxford, England: Macmillan.

Hamp-Lyons, L. (2001). English for academic purposes. In R. Carter & D. Nunan (Eds.), *The Cambridge guide to teaching English to speakers of other languages* (pp. 126–130). Cambridge, England: Cambridge University Press.

Holliday, A. (1994). *Appropriate methodology and social context*. Cambridge, England: Cambridge University Press.

Hyland, K. (2006). *English for academic purposes: An advanced resource book*. London, England: Routledge.

Hyon, S. (2018). *Introducing genre and English for specific purposes*. Abingdon, England: Routledge.

International Civil Aviation Organization. (2004). *Manual on the implementation of ICAO language proficiency requirements*. Montréal, Canada: Author.

Johns, A. M. (2012). The history of English for specific purposes research. In B. Paltridge & S. Starfield (Eds.), *The handbook of English for specific purposes* (pp. 5–30). Oxford, England: Wiley Blackwell.

Johns, T. (1990). From printout to handout: Grammar and vocabulary teaching in the context of data-driven learning. *CALL Austria, 10*, 14–34.

Kostka, I., & Olmstead-Wang, S. (2015). *Teaching English for academic purposes*. Alexandria, VA: TESOL Press.

Liu, J., & Berger, C. M. (2015). *TESOL: A guide*. London, England: Bloomsbury.

MacKenzie, I. (2008). *English for the financial sector: Student's book*. Cambridge, England: Cambridge University Press.

McEnery, T., Xiao, R., & Tono, Y. (2006). *Corpus-based language studies: An advanced resource book*. London, England: Routledge.

Mehta, K., & Dzombak, R. (2013). Ethical decision-making and grassroots diplomacy for social entrepreneurs: Concepts, methodologies and cases. *International Journal of Social Entrepreneurship and Innovation, 2*, 203–224.

Neville, M. (2004). *Beyond the black box: Talk-in-interaction in the airline cockpit*. Aldershot, England: Ashgate.

Pearson, J. (2000). Teaching terminology using electronic resources. In S. Botley, A. McEnery, & A. Wilson (Eds.), *Multilingual corpora in teaching and research* (pp. 92–105). Amsterdam, Netherlands: Rodopi.

Petrescu, M. C., Helms-Park, R., & Dronjic, V. (2017). The impact of frequency and register on cognate facilitation: Comparing Romanian and Vietnamese speakers on the Vocabulary Levels Test. *English for Specific Purposes, 47*, 15–25.

Sarmento, S. (2008). *O uso dos verbos modais em manuais de aviação em inglês: Um estudo baseado em corpus* [The use of modal verbs in aviation manuals: A corpus-based study] (Unpublished doctoral dissertation). Federal University of Rio Grande do Sul, Porto Alegre, Brazil.

Shawcross, P. (1992). *English for aircraft maintenance.* Paris, France: Belin.

Spiro, J. (2013). *Changing methodologies in TESOL.* Edinburgh, Scotland: Edinburgh University Press.

Swales, J. (1990). *Genre analysis: English in academic and research settings.* Cambridge, England: Cambridge University Press.

Viana, V. (2010). Authentic English through the computer: Corpora in the ESOL writing classroom. In S. Kasten (Ed.), *Effective second language writing* (pp. 163–168). Alexandria, VA: TESOL Press.

Viana, V. (2015). Students as researchers: Investigating language appropriateness through corpora. In M. Lewis & H. Reinders (Eds.), *New ways in teaching adults* (2nd ed., pp. 174–177). Alexandria, VA: TESOL Press.

Viana, V. (in press). *New ways in teaching with corpora.* Alexandria, VA: TESOL Press.

Viana, V., Zyngier, S., & Barnbrook, G. (Eds.). (2011). *Perspectives on corpus linguistics.* Amsterdam, Netherlands: John Benjamins.

Woodrow, L. (2018). *Introducing course design in English for specific purposes.* Abingdon, England: Routledge.